Activities
to help Young People deal with
Stress
& Anxiety

Activities

to help Young People deal with

Stress
& Anxiety

Stephanie George

LOGGERHEAD
PUBLISHING

Published in 2015 by
Loggerhead Publishing Ltd, PO Box 928, Northampton NN7 9AP, United Kingdom
Tel: 01604 870828
International Tel: +44 1604 870828
Fax: 01604 870986
International Fax: +44 1604 870986
www.loggerheadpublishing.co.uk

Printed in the United Kingdom.
Designed by Moo Creative (Luton)

British Library Cataloguing in Publication Data. A catalogue record for this book is available from the British Library

ISBN 978-1-909380-86-8

Contents

About the author

Stephanie George is a deputy headteacher based in London. She is also a writer and her book *The Learning Mentor Manual* (Sage, 2010), is the leading educational textbook on Learning Mentor Practice in England. Stephanie is also the author of the books *Activities for Mentoring Young People* (Loggerhead Publishing, 2013), *Activities to Help Young People Deal with Anger* (Loggerhead Publishing, 2014) and co-author of *Activities to Help Young People Deal with Bullying* (Loggerhead Publishing, 2014). She has experience of working with teams of Pastoral Leaders, Heads of Year, Inclusion Teams and Learning Mentors in a variety of challenging settings across the United Kingdom. Stephanie has been responsible for the training and development of Learning Mentors since their inception in 1999. She regularly runs courses and INSET on all aspects of mentoring and intervention practice in educational settings throughout the UK and has trained over 1,000 Learning Mentors.

In 2013 Stephanie and her team were awarded the Times Educational Supplement Award for Support Team of the Year.

Acknowledgements

I am fortunate and blessed to be given the opportunity of writing, an activity which I enjoy and embrace each time I sit down to write. I hope that the work that I am developing and producing here goes some way towards improving the outcomes for the children and young people we work with.

To that end I must thank Catherine McAllister, my publisher, for giving me the opportunity and Sue Christelow for all of her help in jollying me along, editing, indexing and final preparations.

To Jeba Begum, my trusted critic and friend for being a sounding board.

To my lovely sisters Jackie, Joanie and Jennie. To my beloved Gracie and Josh.

Thank you to my wonderful parents, Mr & Mrs George, whose total belief in what I do never fades.

Introduction

There is real pressure on our young people these days – social media, telephones, internet, friendships, peer groups, parents, school demands, exams and teacher pressure can come in many forms and affect many areas of their lives. When pressure turns to stress we need to take note as stress can have undesirable consequences for young people (and adults) who have so much to manage and juggle at a time of intense physical and emotional change. This book is about helping young people to manage stress and anxiety.

Should you have any concerns about the severity of the stress and/or anxiety of the young person that you are working with please seek further specialist advice. Please follow the safeguarding procedures of the organisation within which you work.

This book is intended for use by those working in a variety of settings including schools, alternative education settings, Learning Support Units, Student and Pupil Referral Units, Isolation Units, Exclusion Rooms, youth clubs, community groups and similar settings. The book can be used with students from the ages of 10 to 11 in the upper primary phase through to the upper secondary phase of 15 to 18 years of age.

The activities can be led by teachers, behaviour mentors, pastoral assistants, learning mentors, isolation room leaders and special educational needs staff.

Within this book there are 20 Stress and Anxiety Management activities that cross the bridge between the pastoral and curriculum aspects of learning. They are all cross-referenced with Ofsted's Spiritual, Moral, Social and Cultural Development (SMSC) criteria.

Best practice tells us that a holistic and all-encompassing view of the student is paramount and the pastoral and curriculum aspects of learning should have synergy. We only have to look at the outcomes of the most successful schools to observe this. One without the other does not serve the needs of our young people well. This book is about the whole person and supports the student during periods of difficulty.

The activities can be used in PSHE lessons, circle time, one-to-one sessions, small group and mentoring sessions.

The resources and activities in this book aim to help you to help the young people that you are working with by ultimately focusing upon one thing – their achievement.

How to use this book

The objective of this book is to give practitioners a range of resources that can be used during interventions, be it one to one, workshop or larger groups. Each activity is mapped specifically against Ofsted's Spiritual, Moral, Social and Cultural (SMSC) development criteria (Ofsted Evaluation Framework September 2014 onwards), and the SMSC development criteria applicable is indicated for each activity. A workbook is provided at the end of the book to track the use of each activity to assist with evaluation; this is also a useful resource for providing feedback and evidence of intervention. In addition it offers an opportunity for self-reflection for the student.

The activities address key aspects of the social learning curriculum, in particular:

- Addressing students' approach to difficult and challenging situations

- Addressing students' relationships with others

- Considering students' progress relative to their starting points

- Addressing students' listening and communication skills

- Encouraging consistently high expectations of students

- Giving constructive feedback so as to contribute to students' learning and social development.

The activities are structured in the following way:

1. Activity Objective

2. Intended Audience

3. SMSC Criteria/Ofsted Criteria

4. Context

5. Activity Instructions

6. Closing the Activity

All of the activities have accompanying activity sheets, which are numbered. They can be used discretely as standalone activities.

At the very heart of this book is a set of activities that enable practitioners to demonstrate the impact of intervention.

Most importantly, the activities, once complete, will provide you with evidence of work with students that is demonstrable to them and other stakeholders be they parents, governors, management teams or Ofsted.

Ofsted Evaluation Schedule September 2014

Defining Spiritual, Moral, Social and Cultural Development

Pupils' spiritual development is demonstrated by their:

- Beliefs, religious or otherwise, which inform their perspective on life and their interest in and respect for other people's feelings and values

- Sense of enjoyment and fascination in learning about themselves, others and the world around them

- Use of imagination and creativity in their learning

- Willingness to reflect on their experiences

Pupils' moral development is shown by their:

- Ability to recognise the difference between right and wrong and their readiness to apply this understanding in their own lives

- Understanding the consequences of their actions

- Interest in investigating, and offering reasoned views about moral and ethical issues

Pupils' social development is shown by their:

- Use of a range of social skills in different contexts, including working and socialising with pupils from different religious, ethnic and socio-economic backgrounds

- Willingness to participate in a variety of social settings, cooperating well with others and being able to resolve conflicts effectively

- Interest in, and understanding of, the way communities and societies function

Pupils' cultural development is indicated by their:

- Understanding and appreciation of the wide range of cultural influences that have shaped their own heritage

- Willingness to participate in and respond to artistic, musical, sporting, mathematical, technological, scientific and cultural opportunities

- Interest in exploring and showing respect for cultural diversity as demonstrated by their attitudes towards different religious, ethnic and socio-economic groups in the local, national and global communities

Stress – What is it?

Activity Objective

To give students the opportunity to examine the question "What is Stress?"

Intended Audience

Individual

Spiritual, Moral, Social and Cultural Development Criteria

• Willingness to reflect on their experiences.

Context

In moments of stress there are physical responses and the flight-or-fight response is present. This activity gives the students an opportunity think about where they feel stressed and raises awareness of the physical aspects.

Activity Instructions

1) Lead the student through Activity Sheet 1. Ask the student to note their physical responses and reactions.

2) Lead the student through Activity Sheet 2. What happens after these responses and how might they manage these responses?

Closing the Activity

Close the activity by cementing the suggestion of being aware of what physical reactions might occur if the student found themselves in a similar situation.

What is Stress?

What is Stress? Stress is a normal response to a threatening situation. It is your body preparing itself to a perceived threat. However, prolonged stress is unhealthy.

When I am stressed I feel ...

When I am stressed I feel ...

When I am stressed I feel ...

Responses

Stress		
Pressure	Strenuous	Difficulty
Bother	Hurried	Tough
Challenging	Strain	Demanding
Fast	Trying	Stimulating
Hassle	Arduous	
Problematic	Exciting	

Anxiety – What is it?

Activity Objective

To give students the opportunity to examine "What is Anxiety?"

Intended Audience

Individual

Spiritual, Moral, Social and Cultural Development Criteria

• Willingness to reflect on their experiences.

Context

In moments of stress there are physical responses and the flight-or-fight response is present. This activity gives the students an opportunity think about where they feel stressed and raises awareness of the physical aspects. Anxiety, however, is a persistent worry that does not leave the individual. It is a cause for concern and expert help should be sought where anxiety is prolonged and there are other physical symptoms such as panic attacks.

Activity Instructions

1) Lead the student through Activity Sheet 3. Ask the student to note their physical responses and reactions.

2) Lead the student through Activity Sheet 4. What happens after these responses and how might they manage these responses?

Closing the Activity

Close the activity by cementing the suggestion of being aware of what physical reactions might occur if the student found themselves in a similar situation.

What is Anxiety?

What is Anxiety? Anxiety is a feeling of apprehension, fear or worry that persists after the stressor has abated.

> **When I am anxious I ...**

> **When I am anxious I ...**

> **When I am anxious I ...**

Responses

Anxiety		
Distress	Suffering	Worry
Panic	Disquiet	Apprehension
Agony	Tension	Unease
Angst	Fretfulness	Jumpiness
Struggle	Fear	
Pain	Nervousness	

Stress and Anxiety Initial Self-Assessment

Activity Objective

To give students the opportunity to assess themselves in order to provide a baseline for measuring progress with a focus on relating to others and issues of conflict.

Intended Audience

Individual

Spiritual, Moral, Social and Cultural Development Criteria

- Ability to recognise the difference between right and wrong and their readiness to apply this understanding in their own lives.

- Understanding the consequences of their actions.

- Interest in investigating and offering reasoned views about moral and ethical issues.

Context

The key thing here is to obtain the student's opinion about their own progress, promoting ownership for the student of that progress.

Activity Instructions

1. The questionnaire is appealing to students. I find that they enjoy 'rating themselves'. Allow the student time to work through the Initial Self-Assessment Form (Activity Sheet 5).

2. Review the form and assessment scores as a basis for discussion.

Closing the Activity

Close the activity by logging the evidence in the Student Feedback and Tracking Workbook.

Initial Self-Assessment Form – Stress

Name of Student		Form	
Mentor		Date	

Please circle one box which best describes you. 1 is low and 10 is high

		LOW RATING → HIGH RATING										
1.	Poor concentration	1	2	3	4	5	6	7	8	9	10	Good concentration
2.	Poor punctuality	1	2	3	4	5	6	7	8	9	10	Excellent punctuality
3.	Unhappy	1	2	3	4	5	6	7	8	9	10	Happy
4.	Often angry	1	2	3	4	5	6	7	8	9	10	Peaceful – slow to become angry
5.	Disorganised	1	2	3	4	5	6	7	8	9	10	Well organised
6.	Often tired, even after resting	1	2	3	4	5	6	7	8	9	10	Alert after resting. Rarely complain of tiredness
7.	Issues with keeping friends	1	2	3	4	5	6	7	8	9	10	Popular, have lots of friends
8.	Irritable	1	2	3	4	5	6	7	8	9	10	Rarely irritated
9.	Overwhelmed by deadlines	1	2	3	4	5	6	7	8	9	10	Manage to meet deadlines
10.	Frequently ill and feeling low	1	2	3	4	5	6	7	8	9	10	Not often ill nor feel low
	Totals – Add up all the scores											OUT OF 100

Target Setting and Action Planning

Activity Objective

To develop a set of SMART targets and create a plan of action.

Intended Audience

Individual

Spiritual, Moral, Social and Cultural Development Criteria

- Willingness to reflect on their experiences.

- Use of imagination and creativity in their learning.

Context

Best practice in supportive interventions requires target setting and action planning with the student, as the student needs to plan how they will make progress and what they need to do to get there. The action plan should have SMART features, i.e. it should be Specific, Measurable, Achievable, Realistic and Time focused.

Activity Instructions

1. Stimulate a discussion around target setting with the student – what are the issues that need to be addressed? A focused discussion about the issues affecting learning and achievement needs to take place (use Activity Sheet 6). Prompt the student to then identify the issues affecting learning and achievement. Some aspects to consider during the discussion are:

a) School report

b) Grades – current and forecast

c) Approach to learning and effect

d) Any marked discrepancies between subjects

e) Punctuality

f) Attendance

g) Relationships with staff

h) Relationship with peers

i) Support from home

2. Having had a discussion with the student and developed an area to work on, it is time to set a target and create a plan of action. The plan on Activity Sheet 7 includes the following elements:

a) What does the student wish to achieve?

b) When does the student wish to achieve this?

c) How will the student achieve this?

d) Who will help the student with this?

e) How will the student know that the goal has been achieved? (What evidence will be seen?)

The plan should now be SMART.

Closing the Activity

Review the plan with the student, makc any changes to the draft and then finalise the plan.

Issues Affecting My Learning and Achievement

Issues affecting my learning and achievement are:-
1.
2.
3.
4.
5.

SMART Target Setting and Action Plan

Date	Student Name				Class/Form
What do I want to achieve? (TARGET)	**When do I want to achieve it?**	**How will I achieve my goals?**	**Who will help me with this?**	**How will I know I have achieved my goal? (EVIDENCE)**	
Qualitative Aspect:					
Quantitative Aspect:					

A Letter from School

Activity Objective

For students to recognise how disorganisation can have an impact upon achievement and readiness for learning.

Intended Audience

Individual or small group setting

Spiritual, Moral, Social and Cultural Development Criteria

- Willingness to reflect on their experiences.

- Willingness to participate in a variety of social settings, cooperating well with others and being able to resolve conflicts effectively.

- Ability to recognise the difference between right and wrong and their readiness to apply this understanding in their own lives.

Context

Students are bombarded with deadlines, lots of them. In the secondary setting a young person may have up to 30 lessons or periods in a week. With that goes a number of completion deadlines and the skill of organisation is needed to ensure that deadlines are met, essays are drafted, written and submitted.

Activity Instructions

1. Ask the student(s) to read through the letter or alternatively this can be done together to differentiate and scaffold the activity (Activity Sheet 8).

2. Note down the reactions to the comments made in the letter, asking the student(s) to annotate their response to each point (Activity Sheet 9).

3. Lead a discussion around how you might help the young person(s) and what response you might want to consider giving to the school.

Closing the Activity

Review with the student(s) particularly thinking about what kind of letter they would prefer to receive from school.

A letter from School

The School Office
The High Street
Spring Town
England

Dear Parent/Carer

I am writing to you with regard to the increasingly difficult behaviour being exhibited by your child at this school both in and out of lessons.

We are very concerned about this behaviour as it is now having a detrimental effect upon the learning of other students in the school and to the learning and progress of your child.

In the past week the following events have occurred:

- Arriving at lessons without the correct equipment

- Not completing homework

- Truancy of two English lessons

- Constantly asking to leave lessons to use the toilet.

We are becoming increasingly concerned about your child's disorganised approach and would ask that you make an appointment to come into school to discuss this matter.

Yours faithfully,

Mrs Smith

Head of Year 10

Analysing the letter

1. Arriving at lessons without the correct equipment

2. Not completing homework

3. Truancy of two English lessons

4. Constantly asking to leave lessons to use the toilet

My Stress Signs

Activity Objective

For students to recognise the initial signs of stress and identify some ways of defusing the stress.

Intended Audience

Individual or small group setting

Spiritual, Moral, Social and Cultural Development Criteria

- Willingness to reflect on their experiences.

- Willingness to participate in a variety of social settings, cooperating well with others and being able to resolve conflicts effectively.

Context

Sometimes students become anxious in school and this stress can cause issues in the context of teaching and learning if left unmanaged. This activity is about helping students to recognise that they are becoming stressed and to then identify some ways of dealing with the signs of stress.

Activity Instructions

1. Lead the student(s) through Activity Sheet 10, using the examples given as prompts.

2. Ask the student(s) to suggest their own reasons for becoming stressed. Work through the 'Beginning to Think about What I Do When I Feel Stressed' statements in Activity Sheet 11.

3. Use Activity Sheet 12 to walk the student through some of the strategies to try when they feel stressed.

Closing the Activity

Review the activity with a discussion by summarising the Anxiety Triggers and encouraging self-reflection.

10 Activity Sheet

Beginning to think about why I become stressed

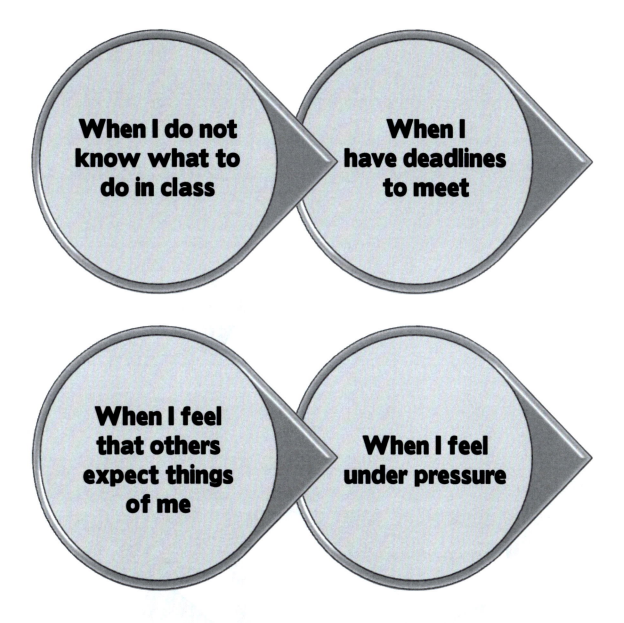

When I do not know what to do in class

When I have deadlines to meet

When I feel that others expect things of me

When I feel under pressure

Beginning to think about ...

What I do when I feel stressed

/ ...

/ ...

/ ...

/ ...

/ ...

/ ...

Ways of Defusing Stress

Strategy	Tried this on (Date)	Outcome when I tried this strategy
Meditation		
Deep breathing		
Asking for help		
Exercise		
Listening to music		
Changing my surroundings		

Ways of Coping

Activity Objective

For students to generate ways of coping in moments of crisis.

Intended Audience

Individual or small group setting

Spiritual, Moral, Social and Cultural Development Criteria

- Willingness to reflect on their experiences.

- Willingness to participate in a variety of social settings, cooperating well with others and being able to resolve conflicts effectively.

Context

The busy school environment can trigger some undesirable responses. Here we think about what to do when things start to become challenging.

Activity Instructions

1. Lead a discussion on ways of coping and work through 'Coping Strategies' (Activity Sheet 13).

2. Lead the students through the "Commitment to Myself" sheet (Activity Sheet 14).

3. Activity Sheet 15 is a prompt sheet to scaffold the learning in this activity that you can use to prompt the student(s).

Closing the Activity

Review with the student(s) where and when they can get help in a crisis or any given situation.

Coping Strategies – Generating ways of coping with stress

I could

I could

I could

Coping Strategies – Generating ways of coping with stress prompt sheet

Meditate	Go for a run	Take deep breaths
Sing	Start keeping a journal	Buy yourself some flowers
Make a gift for someone	Go for a walk	Write a letter to yourself
Light a candle	Take a bath	Give someone a hug
Call a friend	Rest with your legs up against a wall and your back on the floor	
Dance	Cook a healthy meal	

A commitment to myself

> **I will ...**

> **I will ...**

> **I will ...**

Dilemma 1

Activity Objective

To give students the opportunity to consider a dilemma-based learning situation.

Intended Audience

Individual or small groups

Spiritual, Moral, Social and Cultural Development Criteria

- Willingness to reflect on their experiences.

- Willingness to participate in a variety of social settings, cooperating well with others and being able to resolve conflicts effectively.

- Interest in investigating and offering reasoned views about moral and ethical issues.

Context

Students are often faced with dilemmas which can be challenging and emotionally charged. This activity helps to develop a range of thinking skills to address these challenges.

Activity Instructions

1. Lead the students through the dilemma (Activity Sheet 16), asking them to consider their responses.

2. Lead the student through the dilemma again, this time asking if there is an alternative way of responding to the situation, thus encouraging further thinking.

Closing the Activity

Close the activity by asking the students to consider what would be the ideal response if they found themselves in a situation of difficulty.

Dilemma 1

Scenario

Your friend is really worried about not having completed her preparation for a coursework assignment and is aware that she has to give a presentation in front of the class. She has asked you to truant from the lesson with her.

You are also worried about the presentation as you want to get a Grade B for this assignment as you have worked very hard to get to this point from a Grade D at the start of the year.

You are loyal to your friend but you want to get a good grade. You are worried and feel a bit anxious about this situation.

What do you do?

Dilemma 2

Activity Objective

To give students the opportunity to consider a dilemma-based learning situation.

Intended Audience

Individual or small groups

Spiritual, Moral, Social and Cultural Development Criteria

- Willingness to reflect on their experiences.

- Willingness to participate in a variety of social settings, cooperating well with others and being able to resolve conflicts effectively.

- Interest in investigating, and offering reasoned views about moral and ethical issues.

Context

Students are often faced with dilemmas which can be challenging and emotionally charged. This activity helps to develop a range of thinking skills to address these challenges.

Activity Instructions

1. Lead the student(s) through the dilemma (Activity Sheet 17), asking them to consider their responses in this challenging scenario.

   Key question:

   - What would you do? What would you advise a friend to do?

2. Ask the student(s) to create their own dilemma that might be suitable for use with a younger student.

Closing the Activity

Close the activity by reflecting upon the responses and consider when there might be an opportunity to use the activity with a group or pair of younger students.

Dilemma 2

Scenario

A friend of yours has told you that she is feeling overwhelmed by the amount of school work she has to do. Her parents are going through a difficult time and she is very worried that they might split up.

She wants to talk to her mum about this, but she sees her mum very sad a lot of the time and hears her crying at night.

Your friend has started talking about running away from home.

What do you do?

The Stress Matrix

Activity Objective

To give students the opportunity to map their approach to stress and visualise where they are going and where they would like to be.

Intended Audience

Individuals, groups or larger classes

Spiritual, Moral, Social and Cultural Development Criteria

• Willingness to reflect on their experiences.

Context

This activity aims to put into context the ability of the student(s) to change and to place a marker on their willingness to move forward.

Activity Instructions

1) Look at the example given in Activity Sheet 18 which shows two types of students:

a. Student X, who is unable to manage their stress and stresses quickly.

b. Student Y, however, is unable to manage their stress but is slow to stress.

2) Lead the student(s) through the matrix on Activity Sheet 19, explaining what each quadrant represents. The aim would eventually be to arrive in the upper right quadrant (low levels of stress and able to manage stress).

Closing the Activity

Close the activity by reviewing where the student(s) would like to be on the matrix eventually.

Examples of Student X and Student Y

Able to Manage Stress		
Unable to Manage Stress	**x**	**y**
	High Levels of Stress	Low Levels of Stress

Stress Matrix

	High Levels of Stress	Low Levels of Stress
Able to Manage Stress		
Unable to Manage Stress		

Great Expectations

Activity Objective

For students to identify and recognise what expectations others may hold of them and how to consider the pressure that such expectations might have.

Intended Audience

Individual or small group settings

Spiritual, Moral, Social and Cultural Development Criteria

- Willingness to reflect on their experiences.

- Beliefs, religious or otherwise, which inform their perspective on life and their interest in and respect for other people's feelings and values.

Context

Students are bombarded with pressure to confirm, to please, to belong. This activity aims to reveal the extent of such pressures and acknowledge them.

Activity Instructions

1. Ask the student(s) to consider the expectations of three different groups of people: Parents, Peers and Teachers. How might their expectations differ? In what ways?

2. Ask the student(s) to note these on Activity Sheet 20, then look at the differences and to consider why the expectations vary or do not vary.

Closing the Activity

Review with the student(s), thinking about what they expect of themselves.

Expectations

Parental Expectations

Teacher Expectations

Peer Expectations

The Perfect Me

Activity Objective

To give students the opportunity to create a 'Perfect Me' version of themselves.

Intended Audience

Individual or small classes

Spiritual, Moral, Social and Cultural Development Criteria

- Willingness to reflect on their experiences.

- Sense of enjoyment and fascination in learning about themselves, others and the world around them, including the intangible.

Context

There are many pressures upon young people to be part of teams, groups or even gangs and sometimes their individuality is compromised. This activity helps the students to consider the perfect version of themselves in a 'blue-skies-thinking' fashion.

Activity Instructions

1. Select from the Perfect Me 'ingredients' list (Activity Sheet 21) or add your own.

2. Lead a discussion about what would be the 'Perfect Me' for the student(s).

Closing the Activity

Lead a discussion about the kinds of activities and behaviours the 'Perfect Me' version of the student(s) might be engaged in or displaying.

The Perfect Me

Willing	Kind	Thoughtful
Generous	Considerate	Friendly
Good listener	Caring	Straightforward
Honest	Reliable	Understanding
Motivated	Strong	Easy-going
Trustworthy	Chatty	Quiet
Relaxed	Outgoing	Reserved
Informal	Distant	Detached

How I Feel

Activity Objective

To give students the opportunity to reflect upon the physical responses to stress.

Intended Audience

Individual

Spiritual, Moral, Social and Cultural Development Criteria

• Willingness to reflect on their experiences.

Context

In moments of stress there are physical responses and the flight-or-fight response is present. This activity gives the students an opportunity think about where they feel stressed and raises awareness of the physical aspects.

Activity Instructions

1) Lead the student through Activity Sheet 22. Ask the student to note their physical responses and reactions.

2) Lead the student through discussion about this and how they might manage these physical reactions. Use Activity Sheet 23 as a prompt sheet.

Closing the Activity

Close the activity by cementing the suggestion of being aware of what physical reactions might occur if the student found themselves in a similar situation.

How I Feel

What happens to your voice?

What happens to your hands?

What happens to your face?

What happens to you inside?

What happens to your breathing?

Physical Reactions

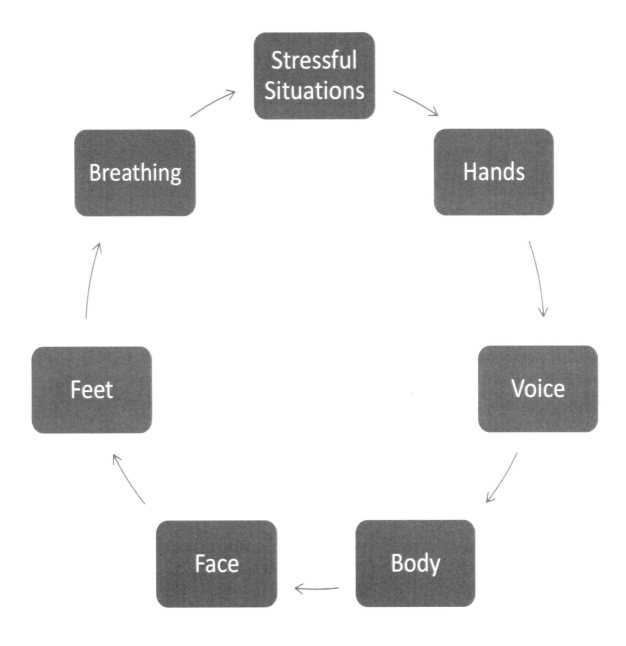

I Feel Good

Activity Objective

To give students the opportunity to stop and take a moment to think about themselves and taking care of themselves.

Intended Audience

Individual, small groups or class

Spiritual, Moral, Social and Cultural Development Criteria

- Willingness to reflect on their experiences.

- Sense of enjoyment and fascination in learning about themselves, others and the world around them, including the intangible.

- Interest in investigating and offering reasoned views about moral and ethical issues.

Context

Students are often faced with a variety of situations that are sometimes overwhelming. Here we think of ways to stop and say "I Feel Good".

Activity Instructions

1. Ask the student(s) to think of some of their own accomplishments. Use Activity Sheet 24 as a prompt.

2. Ask the student(s) to create an 'I Feel Good Montage to Me' (Activity Sheet 25) with all of their accomplishments listed, pictured and drawn on.

3. Encourage the student(s) to use it frequently to remind themselves how great they really are.

Closing the Activity

The 'I Feel Good Montage to Me' is a great stimulus to encourage others. Remind the student(s) that they too can help another.

Accomplishments

Sports Team Captain

I babysit my little sister every Saturday

  ME

I make dinner at home once a week

I got an A in my last English essay

My Accomplishments

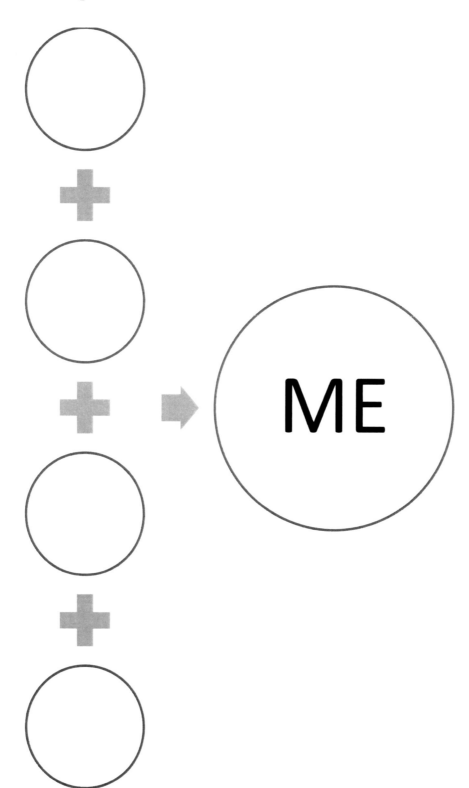

Meditation

Activity Objective

To give students a strategy to still the mind, using meditation, when they feel stressed or need to calm themselves and refocus.

Intended Audience

Individual, pair or group

Spiritual, Moral, Social and Cultural Development Criteria

- Understanding the consequences of their actions.

- Willingness to participate in a variety of social settings, cooperating well with others and being able to resolve conflicts effectively.

Context

In a busy school day a student is surrounded by noise and activity. This in itself can be a cause of stress for a troubled young person. The meditation here is effective in helping to calm and still the mind.

Activity Instructions

Find a quiet place that is without disruption and is comfortable. Talk the student(s) through the meditation using Activity Sheet 26.

Closing the Activity

Encourage the student(s) to revisit the techniques of the meditation whenever they feel the need for a break or quiet time.

Meditation

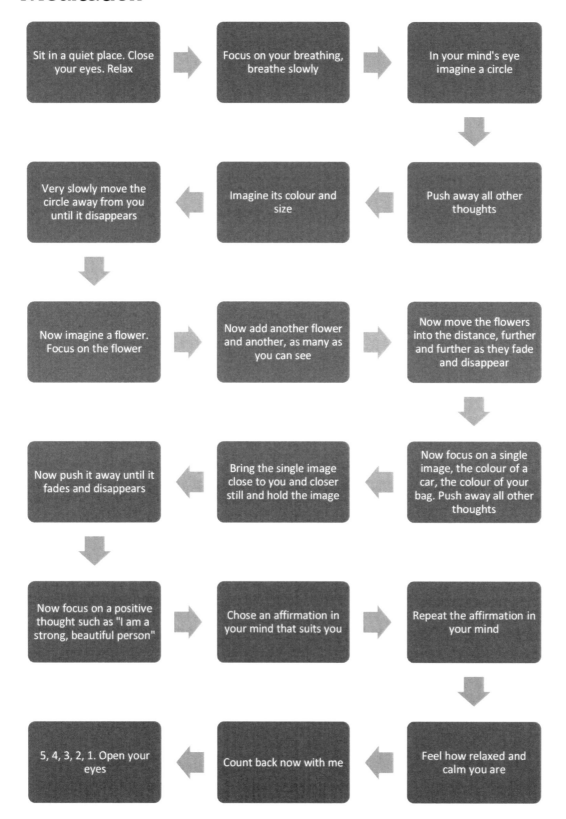

Sit in a quiet place. Close your eyes. Relax	Focus on your breathing, breathe slowly	In your mind's eye imagine a circle
Very slowly move the circle away from you until it disappears	Imagine its colour and size	Push away all other thoughts
Now imagine a flower. Focus on the flower	Now add another flower and another, as many as you can see	Now move the flowers into the distance, further and further as they fade and disappear
Now push it away until it fades and disappears	Bring the single image close to you and closer still and hold the image	Now focus on a single image, the colour of a car, the colour of your bag. Push away all other thoughts
Now focus on a positive thought such as "I am a strong, beautiful person"	Chose an affirmation in your mind that suits you	Repeat the affirmation in your mind
5, 4, 3, 2, 1. Open your eyes	Count back now with me	Feel how relaxed and calm you are

This is my Life

Activity Objective

The aim of the activity is for the students to plot their own life wishes and desires in a safe and supportive way.

Intended Audience

Individual or small group setting

Spiritual, Moral, Social and Cultural Development Criteria

- Willingness to reflect on their experiences.
- Willingness to participate in a variety of social settings, cooperating well with others and being able to resolve conflicts effectively.

Context

This activity helps the student(s) to put into context that what is happening now in the present will not always be so. Also that things do change and can change rapidly, and they will encounter as they go through life both good times and sad times. We hope to build resilience within the young person and this activity helps them to think about their aspirations and future wishes.

Activity Instructions

1. Lead the student through the activity, describing the events that occur at each step (Activity Sheet 27).
2. Lead the student through the next stage and decide, 'What happens next?' using Activity Sheet 28 as necessary.

Closing the Activity

Review the outcomes with the student(s) and evaluate them using the Student Tracking and Feedback Workbook.

This is my Life

I am 5 years old			
I am 10 years old			
I am 15 years old			
I am 20 years old			
I am 30 years old			

This is my Life Prompts

This is my Life - Prompt sheet	
Moved house	I graduated from university
My cat was ill and she died	I learnt how to swim
I passed my driving test	Moved schools
I cared for my Dad	I left school with top grades
My brother was born	I got my dream job
I won first prize at sports day	I learnt how to play an instrument

It's About Time

Activity Objective

For students to know how to manage their study time effectively.

Intended Audience

Individual or small group setting

Spiritual, Moral, Social and Cultural Development Criteria

- Use of imagination and creativity in their learning.
- Willingness to reflect on their experiences.
- Sense of enjoyment and fascination in learning about themselves, others and the world around them, including the intangible.

Context

For some students managing time can be a challenge and a barrier to learning and achievement. This activity is designed to help students develop skills to manage their time effectively.

Activity Instructions

1. Ask the student(s) to complete the Time Management Questionnaire (Activity Sheet 29).
2. Read the case study 'Plan Claire's Evening' (Activity Sheet 30) and complete 'Organising Claire' (Activity Sheet 31).
3. Now ask the students to have a go at planning their own time using 'Organising My Time' (Activity Sheet 32). Ask the student(s) to plan their weekday evening.
4. Complete the Review Sheet (Activity Sheet 33).

Closing the Activity

Key questions:

- What did we learn today?
- How does planning our time help with organisation?

Ask the student(s) to use the plan one evening this week.

Time Management Questionnaire

Questions:	Responses:			
Do I use time efficiently? YES/NO (If YES, how?)				
How do I waste time?				
What or who distracts me from my work?				
Do I waste time getting started? YES/NO (If YES, how?)				
Do I find the time passes and I don't know what has happened? YES/NO (If YES, how?)				

Plan Claire's Evening

- Claire gets home from school at 4:30pm

- Claire has a chapter of a History book to read: 45 minutes

- A Science problem to sort: 30 minutes

- An English assignment: 30 minutes

- Claire wants to ring her boyfriend: 15 minutes

- Watch two programmes at 6:45-7:15pm and 9:30-10:30pm

- Exercise to a video lasting 45 minutes

- By 6pm she will have had her dinner

- Her parents like her to be in bed by 10:30pm

Organise Claire's evening so that she can do all of these things.

Organising Claire

Use the chart framework to organise Claire's evening

Time	Activity

Organising My Time

Use the chart framework to organise your evening. Think about all of the things you need to achieve and create your own plan.

Time	Activity

Review Sheet

How useful was the plan in helping to manage time?

What issues were encountered using the plan?

What would you change?

A Stress-free Study Place

Activity Objective

To consider the necessary elements for creating a positive environment for successful study.

Intended Audience

Individual or small group setting

Spiritual, Moral, Social and Cultural Development Criteria

• Willingness to reflect on their experiences.

• Use of imagination and creativity in their learning.

Context

As well as good time management, students need a purposeful, appropriate and suitable place to study. This activity aims to help students to have ownership and responsibility in organising their own place to study.

Activity Instructions

1. Brainstorm what are the key things needed to create a successful and productive study environment (Activity Sheet 34).

2. Ask the student(s) to complete the Study Questionnaire (Activity Sheet 35). The purpose of the questionnaire is to get a picture of their current study environment.

3. Arrange to meet the student(s) after the target day has passed. Complete the Study Questionnaire Review (Activity Sheet 36).

Closing the Activity

Review the plan with the student(s) and discuss its impact upon successful study.

Brainstorm – My Ideal Study Space

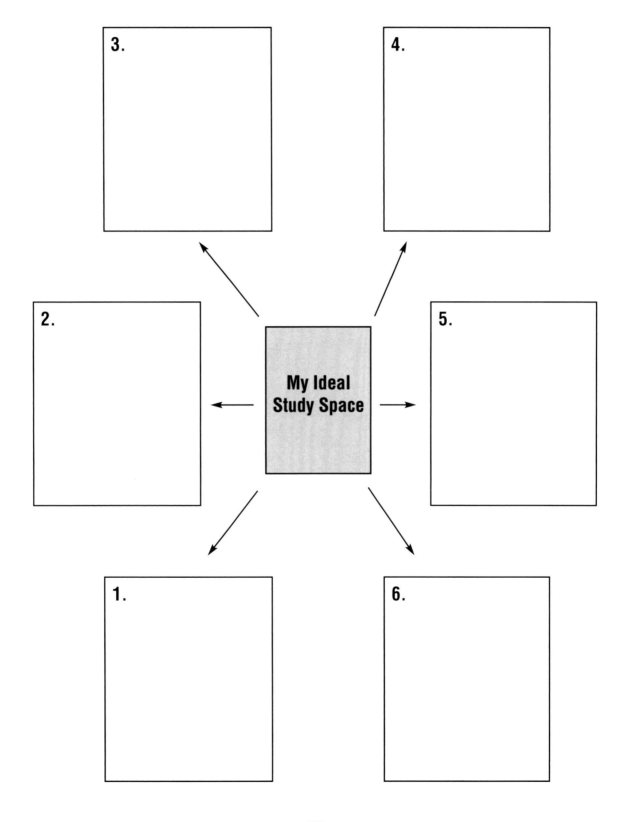

Study Questionnaire

QUESTIONS	YES	NO	ACTION NEEDED	REVIEW DATE
I have a suitable space to study at home				
My study space is free of interruption				
I am often disturbed by the telephone or internet				
I have the appropriate writing equipment and stationery for study				
I have the appropriate textbooks and resources				
I know who to ask if I need help with my work				

Study Questionnaire Review

QUESTIONS	YES	NO	ACTION NEEDED	TARGET DATE	IMPACT OF CHANGE
I have a suitable space to study at home					
My study space is free of interruption					
I am often disturbed by the telephone or internet					
I have the appropriate writing equipment and stationery for study					
I have the appropriate textbooks and resources					
I know who to ask if I need help with my work					

Stress and Anxiety Student Reassessment

Activity Objective

To give students the opportunity to reassess themselves in order to measure progress.

Intended Audience

Individual

Spiritual, Moral, Social and Cultural Development Criteria

- Ability to recognise the difference between right and wrong and their readiness to apply this understanding in their own lives.

- Understanding the consequences of their actions.

- Interest in investigating and offering reasoned views about moral and ethical issues.

Context

This reassessment activity should be undertaken at the end of or at suitable intervals during the intervention process. The 'Initial Self-Assessment' activity should always have been completed first. The reassessment seeks to establish the difference intervention has made in a data driven and quantifiable way.

Activity Instructions

1. The student completes the Reassessment Form (Activity Sheet 37).

2. Provide the Reassessment Form to the student and allow some time to complete it.

3. You will need:

   a) The initial Self-Assessment Form (taken from the activity 'Initial Self-Assessment') completed

   b) The Reassessment Form completed

   c) The Assessment Evaluation Form (Activity Sheet 38)

4. You will need to map the responses for each of the forms onto the Assessment Evaluation Form. You will need to calculate the differences (+ or -). Calculate the total responses for

each category. What you will then have is the difference for each category as a negative or a positive improvement. This data is valuable as you are now able to track the impact of intervention using qualitative questions in a quantitative way.

Closing the Activity

Review the gains and losses for each area.

Key questions:

• What needs further work?

• What is secure?

• What needs further consideration?

Reassessment Form – Stress

Name of Student		Form	
Mentor		Date	

Please circle one box which best describes you. 1 is low and 10 is high

		LOW RATING									HIGH RATING	
1.	Poor concentration	1	2	3	4	5	6	7	8	9	10	Good concentration
2.	Poor punctuality	1	2	3	4	5	6	7	8	9	10	Excellent punctuality
3.	Unhappy	1	2	3	4	5	6	7	8	9	10	Happy
4.	Often angry	1	2	3	4	5	6	7	8	9	10	Peaceful — slow to become angry
5.	Disorganised	1	2	3	4	5	6	7	8	9	10	Well organised
6.	Often tired even after resting	1	2	3	4	5	6	7	8	9	10	Alert after resting. Rarely complain of tiredness
7.	Issues with keeping friends	1	2	3	4	5	6	7	8	9	10	Popular, have lots of friends
8.	Irritable	1	2	3	4	5	6	7	8	9	10	Rarely irritated
9.	Overwhelmed by deadlines	1	2	3	4	5	6	7	8	9	10	Manage to meet deadlines
10.	Frequently ill and feeling low	1	2	3	4	5	6	7	8	9	10	Not often ill or feeling low
	Totals — Add up all the scores											OUT OF 100

Assessment Evaluation Form – Stress

Name of Student		Form	
Mentor		Date	

	BASELINE RATING (Taken from the initial Assessment Form)	REASSESSMENT RATING (Taken from the Reassessment Form)	DIFERRENCE (+/-)
1.			
2.			
3.			
4.			
5.			
6.			
7.			
8.			
9.			
10.			

Date of Baseline	Baseline Score	Reassessment Score	Difference
			+/-

Review of Target Setting and Action Planning

Activity Objective

To review a set of targets and prepare a plan of action.

Intended Audience

Individual

Spiritual, Moral, Social and Cultural Development Criteria

- Understanding of the consequences of their actions.

- Willingness to reflect on their experiences.

Context

This activity is a review of the activity titled 'Target Setting and Action Planning'.

In order for us to know whether an intervention is effective it is crucial that we review any Target Setting and Action Planning that we conduct.

Activity Instructions

You will need the student's original Action Plan. Allow the student to read through and examine this plan. A guided discussion is useful to stimulate thinking. Then using the review grid (Activity Sheet 39), follow the key questions and complete.

Closing the Activity

This activity presents a rich learning opportunity in that it seeks to discover what is the most effective approach based upon the student's prior learning experience and the plan of action that they themselves created.

The evidence gathered from this activity is extremely powerful in that it informs a process for moving forward that is personalised, differentiated and specific to the student's needs.

Review Grid

	Qualitative Aspect	Quantitative Aspect	What future improvement is needed?
EXAMPLE	I am better prepared at the start of the day	My attendance to registration has improved by 5%	I need to improve my attendance to registration by a further 5%
What did I achieve?			
How do I know I have achieved this? (Evidence)			
It would have been better if ...			
I'm happy that I ...			
Next time I will ...			

Student Tracking and Feedback Workbook

Stress and Anxiety Management

Student Name:

Form:

How to use this Tracking and Feedback Workbook

The Tracking and Feedback Workbook can be used to track the implementation of the stress and anxiety activities and their completion. It is also used to assess a student's engagement with the activity, progress and development during the activity, their questions and responses. A rating could be applied as follows in the chart below for assessment and evaluation purposes. At the end of each activity use the workbook to record the student's progress and add comments together with leader feedback.

1	Student disengaged and activity not completed.
2	Student somewhat engaged and activity partially completed.
3	Student engaged and made a positive attempt at completing the activity.
4	Student fully engaged and all of the activity completed.

Date Completed (Write in the date you complete the activity)	Activity Title (Write in the Activity Titles as you complete them, in the order you wish)	Student Evaluation & Comment (Student to write in their comment)	Leader Feedback/Comment (Circle Rating and write in comment)			
			1	2	3	4
			1	2	3	4
			1	2	3	4
			1	2	3	4
			1	2	3	4

Date Completed	Activity Title	Student Evaluation & Comment	Leader Feedback/Comment			
			1	2	3	4
			1	2	3	4
			1	2	3	4
			1	2	3	4
			1	2	3	4

Date Completed	Activity Title	Student Evaluation & Comment	Leader Feedback/Comment			
			1	2	3	4
			1	2	3	4
			1	2	3	4
			1	2	3	4
			1	2	3	4

Date Completed	Activity Title	Student Evaluation & Comment	Leader Feedback/Comment			
			1	2	3	4
			1	2	3	4
			1	2	3	4
			1	2	3	4
			1	2	3	4

Bibliography

Bishop, S (2008), *Running a Nurture Group*, Sage Publications.

Buzan, T (1984), *Use your Memory*, BBC Books.

Canter, L and Canter, M (1977), *Assertive Discipline*, Lee Canter Associates.

Claxton, G (2002), *Building Learning Power: Helping Young People Become Better Learners*, TLO Limited.

Department for Education and Employment (DfEE) (1999), *Social Inclusion: Pupil Support*, Circular 11/99, DfEE Publications.

Department for Education and Skills (DfES) (2004), *Every Child Matters: Change for Children*, Reference 1081/2004, DfES Publications.

Dickinson, C (1996) *Effective Learning Activities*, Network Educational Press.

Egan, G (2001), The Skilled Helper: *A Problem-Management and Opportunity-Development Approach to Helping*, Wadsworth.

George, S (2010), *The Learning Mentor Manual*, Sage Publications.

Hymans, M (2003), *Think Before You Act*, Lucky Duck Publishing.

Lucas, B and Claxton, G (2010), *New Kinds of Smart*, Open University Press.

Rogers, B (2006), *Cracking the Hard Class,* 2nd Edition, Paul Chapman Educational Publishing.

Rogers, CR and Lyon, H (2013), *On Becoming an Effective Teacher: Person-centered teaching, psychology, philosophy, and dialogues*, Routledge.

Zunker, VG (2005), *Career Counseling: A Holistic Approach*, Brooks Cole.

Other Stephanie George Titles from Loggerhead Publishing

Activities to help Young People Deal with Anger

How to address issues relating to anger and conflict using a mentoring approach

By Stephanie George

These activities have a particular focus on developing skills for managing anger, conflict and relating to others. They provide specific, structured tasks that can be used during one-to-one mentoring intervention and for group work.

There are 20 conflict/anger management specific activities that cross the bridge between the pastoral and curriculum aspects of learning. The activities include:

• My Anger Triggers • Anger Matrix • Initial Self-Assessment – Relating to Others • Student Reassessment and Evaluation • How I Feel When I am Angry • Ways of Coping • Improving my Listening • Dilemmas • Conflict – What it is and How to Deal with it • What Happens Next? • Stop Seeing Red • My Autobiography • My Progress • Target Setting and Action Planning • Review

Each activity includes full instructions and any necessary worksheets to photocopy or print out.

74 pages, A4, photocopiable   Ages 10-16
ISBN 978-1-909380-49-3   Ref 104-B   £32.50

Activities for Mentoring Young People

How to engage productively with young people

By Stephanie George

Engaging with young people as a mentor can be difficult but here the author draws on her years of experience to provide tried-and-tested activities that will help. The mentoring activities include:

• Knowing Me, Knowing You
• Planning the Journey
• Initial Self-Assessment
• Target Setting and Action Planning
• Improving Attendance
• Conflict – What it is and How to Deal with it
• I'm Seeing Red/Stop Seeing Red
• It's About Time
• A Place to Study

Essential for learning mentors, behaviour mentors, inclusion teams and SEN teams.

92 pages, A4, photocopiable

Ages 11-16

ISBN 978-1-909380-03-5

Ref 062-B £32.50

Activities to help Young People Deal with Bullying

How to support professionals working with young people on all areas related to bullying

By Stephanie George, Patricia St Louis, Jeba Begum & Jacqueline Morrison

A book of activities to help professionals work through bullying issues with young people, covering:

• The impact of the group • Belonging • Social settings • Norms • Values • Peer groups • Friendships • Power • Isolation • Responsibility • Restorative work • Conciliation work

The activities cover the range of bullying behaviours seen in educational settings such as whether a student is exhibiting bullying behaviours, the role of the bystander, the perception of bullying as a behaviour choice and the impact of bullying upon others. The activities all have accompanying activity sheets to copy and hand out to students. Most of them can be used discretely as stand-alone activities. The book also includes a photocopiable Student Tracking and Feedback Workbook for evaluation and to assess effectiveness.

74 pages, A4, photocopiable   Ages 10-18   ISBN 978-1-909380-52-3   Ref 105-B   £32.50

BUY ALL 4 TITLES IN THE SERIES AT A SAVING
Set of 4 Activities Books on Mentoring, Bullying, Anger and Stress Ref 172-B £123.50

To place an order or for more details please call +44 (0) 1604 870828, email orders@loggerheadpublishing.co.uk or visit www.loggerheadpublishing.co.uk